Don't Bump The Giraffe Knee

By Vincent A. Watson

To my children Jaylen and Maliyah and all the kids around the world:

There's only one you,

God didn't make two

Accept yourself and to yourself always remain true

-DAD/ VAW-

You ever play a game of tag

Between a giraffe legs

It’s such a squeeze

But whatever you do please don’t bump the giraffe knees

If you start to fall you better freeze

And if your nose starts to itch you better not sneeze

And whatever you do please don't bump the giraffe knees

The giraffe legs are tall as trees

You can relax under them and enjoy the cool breeze

You will never see any other legs like these

But whatever you do please don’t bump the giraffe knees

You can slide under them while wearing ski's

And take a picture with a monkey, be sure to say cheese

But whatever you do please don't bump the giraffe knees

You can do jumping jack under the giraffe legs with ease

While sipping on different teas

But please be careful not to bump the giraffe knees

You can swing on a swing set

While trying to catch butterflies in your net

Catch one, two, and three

But whatever you do please don't bump the giraffe knee

You can row a boat like you’re sailing the seven sea’s

All while eating carrots and peas

But whatever you do please don’t bump the giraffe knees

Peas
Carrots

You can buzz like the honeybee’s

While saying your A-B-C’s

But whatever you do please don’t bump the giraffe knees

ABC...

You can do backflips and cartwheels

While playing ball with two friendly seals

Named Louie and Marie

But please- don't bump the giraffe knee

LOUIE
MARIE

You can play the piano mat with a band of fleas

You can dance and step on all the keys

But please - don't bump the giraffe knees

Hey, where did you go?

Are you playing hide and go seek?

Well one thing you should know

Is that giraffe knees are weak

So where are thee?

Are you hiding from me?

Oh, I see

You must've bumped the giraffe knee

www.ingramcontent.com/pod-product-compliance
Lightning Source LLC
Chambersburg PA
CBHW042017110726
48006CB00004B/1128

* 9 7 9 8 2 1 8 2 4 3 0 1 2 *